# HORRID HENRY'S Sticker Book

D1726895

**60 great stickers inside!**

Now a major TV series

Based on the **HORRID HENRY** books by Francesca Simon, illustrated by Tony Ross

Orion Children's Books

# MY DIARY by Henry

**MONDAY**

My teacher, Miss Battle-Axe, says everyone has to keep a diary for one week and write about their family and friends. Yeuch! In my family, there's me, Mum and Dad, and, unfortunately Peter, the slimy toad.
Friends?
Rude Ralph is OK.
Miss Battle-Axe didn't say enemies, but I've got loads!
Enemy number 1 is Moody Margaret.

Add lots of Glop and splats. Henry's diary is very messy!

# TUESDAY

Have to go to school again today. Work, work, work. Ugh! I'm in trouble for poking William, tripping Linda, pinching Andrew, making rude noises and talking in class. Miss Battle-Axe is very angry!

Can you find the best stickers to bring Miss Battle-Axe to life?

# WEDNESDAY

Moody Margaret came to stay last night.
She's driving us all mad! This morning,
she woke us all up with her horrible trumpet.
And she brought three boxes of toys with her
and threw them all over the bathroom!

Henry

22+7 = 49 X
51+21 = 74 X
12+4 = 17 X
6×3 = X
24-5 = 17 X

132 X
2⟌364
7⟌5421
49

Now **YOU** throw Margaret's toys all over the bathroom.

# THURSDAY

Oh no! Horrible, horrible Thursday.
The worst day of the week.
It's class swimming day with Soggy Sid!

Match heads
and bodies.
Have fun
mixing them up!

PETER'S SCHOOL REPORT

It has been a pleasure
teaching Peter this year. He is
polite, hard-working and
co-operative. The best student I
have ever taught.

Behaviour: Perfect

English: Perfect

Maths: Perfect

Science: Perfect

PE: Perfect

HENRY'S SCHOOL REPORT

It has been horrible teaching
Henry this year. He is rude,
lazy and disruptive. The
worst student I have ever
taught.

Behaviour: Horrid

English: Horrid

Maths: Horrid

Science: Horrid

PE: Horrid

# FRIDAY

Hoorah! The weekend starts here. Me and Margaret sneak into the kitchen to make Glop.

Splat as much Glop as you can on this page!

It's brilliant! There's Glop on the ceiling and Glop on the floor, Glop on the clock and Glop on the door.

## SATURDAY

Mum and Dad have decorated smelly Peter's bedroom. They won't decorate mine because they say it's too messy!
I'm helping Peter put everything back into his room — then Mum and Dad will give me some money. Hee hee!

Help Peter put all his belongings back into his bedroom.
You can be neat and tidy like Peter, or messy like Horrid Henry!

# SUNDAY

Mum makes me tidy up my bedroom all evening. It's not fair! I want to watch TV.

Find the jigsaw stickers and complete the picture of Horrid Henry's bedroom.

**Remember: No Glop or splats on this page, as Henry's reward is a gold gizmo for tidying!**